Maximize Your IQ

**Philip J. Carter &
Kenneth A. Russell**

Sterling Publishing Co., Inc.
New York

Library of Congress Cataloging-in-Publication Data

Carter, Philip.

   Maximize your IQ / Philip J. Carter & Kenneth A. Russell.

      p. cm.

   Includes bibliographical references and index.

   ISBN-13: 978-1-4027-3273-7 (alk. paper)

   ISBN-10: 1-4027-3273-2 (alk. paper)

   1. Intelligence tests. 2. Self-evaluation. I. Russell, Kenneth A. II. Title.

BF431.3.C3648 2006

153.9'3—dc22   2006014425

10   9   8   7   6   5   4   3   2   1

Published by Sterling Publishing Co., Inc.

387 Park Avenue South, New York, NY 10016

© 2007 by Philip J. Carter

This book, *Maximize Your IQ*, is based on a work entitled *Improve Your
IQ* published in England © 1995 by Ken Russell and Philip Carter.

Distributed in Canada by Sterling Publishing % Canadian Manda Group

165 Dufferin Street, Toronto, Ontario, Canada M6K 3H6

Distributed in the United Kingdom by GMC Distribution Services

Castle Place, 166 High Street, Lewes, East Sussex, England BN7 1XU

Distributed in Australia by Capricorn Link (Australia) Pty. Ltd.

P.O. Box 704, Windsor, NSW 2756, Australia

Sterling ISBN-13: 978-1-4027-3273-7

        ISBN-10: 1-4027-3273-2

For information about custom editions, special sales, premium and
corporate purchases, please contact Sterling Special Sales
Department at 800-805-5489 or specialsales@sterlingpub.com.

Contents

Introduction

WHAT IS INTELLIGENCE?

Intelligence is the capacity to learn or understand. Every person possesses a single general ability of mind. This ability varies in amount from person to person, but remains approximately the same throughout life for any individual. It is this ability that enables the individual to deal with real situations and profit intellectually from sensory experience.

In psychology, intelligence is more narrowly defined as the capacity to acquire knowledge and understanding and use it in different and new situations. Under test conditions, it's possible to study formally the success of an individual in adapting to a specific situation.

In the formation of intelligence tests (known as IQ tests), most psychologists treat intelligence as a general ability operating as a common factor in a wide variety of aptitudes.

It does not follow, however, that a person who is good at IQ tests is necessarily capable of excelling at academic tests, regardless of how logical and quick-witted that person may be. Motivation and dedication are sometimes more important than brainpower. To score highly on an academic test requires the ability to concentrate on a single subject, obtain an understanding of it, and internalize the material solidly enough to keep the facts in mind during an examination. Often it is difficult for someone with a high IQ to do this because an overactive and inquiring mind cannot focus on one subject for very long and forever wishes to diversify. Such a person would have to apply a high level of self-discipline in order to succeed at academic tests, but if such self-discipline is applied, the individual is likely to obtain a very high mark.

There are many different types of intelligence that can be described as genius, and people who have outstanding artistic, creative, sporting, or practical prowess can all be highly successful without necessarily having a high IQ. It must also be pointed out that having a high IQ also does not mean that one has a good memory. A good memory is yet another type of intelligence that could result in high academic success despite a low measured IQ.

Someone with a rare combination of a high IQ, good memory, self-discipline, and dedication is likely to be a very high flyer indeed.

WHAT IS IQ?

IQ is the abbreviation for Intelligence Quotient. The word "quotient" means the results of dividing one quantity by another. Intelligence is "mental ability," "quickness of mind." It is generally believed that a person's IQ rating is a hereditary characteristic and barely changes throughout life, tailing off with old age.

When measuring the IQ of a child, the child would attempt an intelligence test which has been standardized, with the average score recorded for each age group. Thus a child of ten years of age who scored the results expected of a child of twelve would have an IQ calculated as follows:

$$\frac{\text{MENTAL AGE}}{\text{CHRONOLOGICAL AGE}} \times 100 = \text{IQ RATING}$$

$$\frac{12 \text{ YEARS OLD}}{10 \text{ YEARS OLD}} \times 100 = 120 \text{ IQ RATING}$$

This method would not, however, apply to adults, whose assessment would be made according to known percentages of the population.

WHAT IS AN INTELLIGENCE TEST?

In contrast to specific proficiencies or aptitudes, intelligence tests (IQ tests) are standardized examinations devised to measure human intelligence as distinct from attainments. A test consists of a series of questions, exercises, and/or tasks which have been set to many thousands of examinees and for which, in the case of children, normal scores have been worked out for each year of life the test is designed to cover. Intelligence tests may be individual or group. An individual test is given to only one examinee at a time and requires a highly qualified examiner. A group test can be given to a considerable number of examinees at one time but does not have the refined accuracy of the individual test.

There are a number of different types of intelligence test— Stanford-Binet, Cattell, and Wechsler, for example—and each has its own scales of intelligence. The Stanford-Binet test, widely used in the United States, is heavily weighted with questions involving verbal abilities; the Cattell test, used by British Mensa, uses two tests, one having a high verbal content and the other culture-fair (diagrams only); the Wechsler scales consist of two separate verbal and performance subscales, each with its own IQ.

It's said that to have a mastery of words is to have in one's possession the ability to produce order out of chaos, and that command of vocabulary is a true measure of intelligence. As such, vocabulary tests are widely used in intelligence testing. There has been, however, a swing toward diagrammatic tests, where logic rather than word knowledge is important. These tests include a large proportion of spatial questions. Advocates of this type of test argue that diagrammatic tests are culture-fair and test raw intelligence without the influence of prior knowledge. They are designed to probe an individual's understanding of space relationships and design. We have included a high percentage of this type of question in the tests that follow.

Improve Your IQ

It is generally agreed that IQ is hereditary and remains fairly constant throughout life. Is it possible, therefore, to improve one's performance on IQ tests? Some years ago one of the authors of this book successfully applied for membership in the high-IQ society Mensa by improving his IQ rating by six points over a twelve-month period by constant practice on IQ tests. We believe that, through practice on different types of IQ test and attuning your mind to the different types of question that may be encountered, it is possible to improve IQ, if only by a few vital percentage points. These few percentage points, however, may prove crucial in increasing job prospects and mean the difference between success or failure when job interviews include the taking of an IQ test.

A gymnast improves performance and increases chances of success at whatever level of competition by means of punishing training schedules and refinement of technique. In the same way, the mental gymnastics in this book will give you the opportunity to increase your performance on IQ tests.

TYPES OF QUESTION

While there's no substitute for practicing on actual tests, it's useful to have prior understanding of the types of question that may be encountered.

The following are typical examples of vocabulary questions used in IQ tests:

Classification

These are questions where a list of words is given and you have to choose the "odd one out."

Example: globe, orb, sphere, scepter, ball

Answer: Scepter is the odd one out, since the others are all circular objects.

Synonyms

A synonym is a word having the same meaning as another of the same language.

Example 1: Which word in the brackets means the same as the word in capital letters?

AVERAGE (poor, mean, public, weak, value)

Answer: mean

Example 2: Which two words are the closest in meaning?

walk, run, drive, stroll, fly, sit

Answer: walk, stroll

Antonyms

An antonym is a word having a meaning opposite to another of the same language.

Example 1: Which word in the brackets means the opposite of the word in capital letters?

CARELESS (exact, mindful, strict, anxious, dutiful)

Answer: mindful

Example 2: Which two words are opposite in meaning?

curved, long, big, small, broad, fat

Answer: big, small

Analogy

An analogy is a similitude of relations, where it is necessary to reason the answer from a parallel case.

Example: OASIS is to SAND as

ISLAND is to sea, river, water, waves, pond

Answer: Water, because an oasis is surrounded by sand and an island is surrounded by water.

Double meanings

These are designed to test your ability to find quickly alternative meanings of words. You are looking for a word having the same meaning as the two definitions provided.

Example: give account of (. . . .) noise from a gun

Answer: report

Double words

In this test you are given the first part of a word or phrase and you have to find the second part. The same second part then becomes the first part of a second word or phrase.

Example: MEAN (. . . .) PIECE

Answer: TIME: to make meantime and timepiece.

Anagrams

Example 1: Which of these is not a vegetable?

UFEFTELR
CNSIAHP
NOARCAI
SPRIAPN

Answer: NOARCAI is an anagram of OCARINA, which is a small wind instrument. The vegetables are truffle, spinach, parsnip.

Example 2: Solve the anagram (one word):

BARE SMILE

Answer: miserable

Code words

Example: Which word goes in the brackets?

PILOT (LATE) PLACE
LIMIT (. . . .) SPINE
L I T E

Answer: MITE. The word in the brackets is formed in this way: the first letter is the third letter of the left-hand word. The second letter is the third letter of the right-hand word. The third letter is the fifth letter of the left-hand word, and the fourth letter is the fifth letter of the right-hand word.

Preceding letters

Example: Find a four-letter word that forms a different word with each preceding letter or letters.

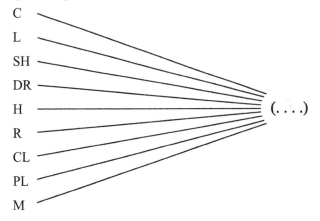

C
L
SH
DR
H   (. . . .)
R
CL
PL
M

Answer: OVER, to produce cover, lover, shover, drover, hover, rover, clover, plover, and mover.

The list above is, of course, by no means complete. There are a number of unique question types in which it is necessary to apply logical thought and lateral thinking. The tests that follow include several examples designed to provide practice in applying the logical thought processes necessary to solve such questions.

The following are some typical non-vocabulary (spatial) questions used in IQ tests:

Matrix

Usually an array of nine squares is presented with the bottom right-hand square empty, and you are asked to choose from a list of options. It is necessary to study the array as a whole, or look across each horizontal line and down each vertical line, to work out the logical pattern or progression that is occurring.

Example:

Answer: Each row and each column contains a circle, a square, and a triangle.

Also, each row and column contains a black, white, and shaded figure.

Odd one out

Example: Which of these figures is the odd one out?

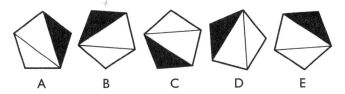

| A | B | C | D | E |

Answer: B, the other four are all the same figure but are rotated.

Analogy

Example:

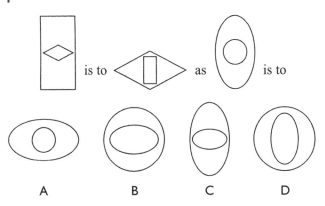

is to ... as ... is to

| A | B | C | D |

Answer: D, the rectangle stays upright but gets smaller. It goes inside the diamond, which gets bigger. So, the ellipse stays upright but gets smaller and goes inside the circle, which gets bigger.

Sequence

Example: Which of the choices below comes next in the above sequence?

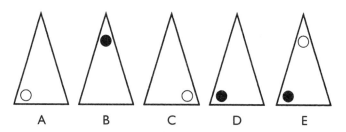

| A | B | C | D | E |

Answer: D, the dot visits each angle of the triangle in turn, traveling counterclockwise, and is black, then white, in turn.

As with the verbal examples, this is by no means a complete list but a selection of the types of question you may encounter. There will, of course, be many different variations of these examples, many different question types and unique type questions, where it is also necessary to apply logical thought and lateral thinking.

HOW IMPORTANT IS IQ?

Cynics will say that the only thing having a high-IQ proves is that the individual has scored well on an intelligence test. It remains, however, that an IQ test is the only known and tried method of measuring intelligence. Some technical weaknesses do exist in all tests, so it is crucial that results be viewed as only one kind of information about an individual. Nevertheless it must be stressed how commonplace IQ tests have become, and that proficiency at IQ tests can significantly improve one's employment prospects and give an individual a better start in one's chosen career.

Although desirable, a high IQ is not the only key to success. Characteristics such as ambition, personality, temperament, and even compassion are also, perhaps even more, essential.

How to Use This Book

This book consists of eight separate tests, made up of forty questions each, for you to work through. The difficulty level of the tests is approximately the same. Each test is given an approximate IQ rating. There is also an accumulative rating for all eight tests.

A time limit of ninety minutes is allowed for each test. The correct answers are given at the end of each test—award yourself one point for each correct answer. Some answers will include an explanation, allowing you to review the question with a new eye if you came up with the wrong answer.

Use the following tables to assess your IQ:

One Test:

SCORE	RATING	APPROX. IQ RATING
36–40	Exceptional	140+
31–35	Excellent	131–140
25–30	Very good	121–130
19–24	Good	111–120
14–18	Average	90–110

Eight Tests:

SCORE	RATING	APPROX. IQ RATING
281–320	Exceptional	140+
241–280	Excellent	131–140
193–240	Very good	121–130
145–192	Good	111–120
112–144	Average	90–110

Test One

1. Which is the odd one out?

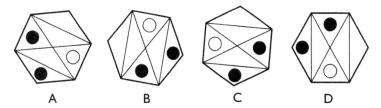

| A | B | C | D |

2. Which two words that sound alike but are spelled differently mean:

   (a) pretense
   (b) dim

3. What creature should go in the brackets reading downward so as to convert the letters to the left of the brackets into three-letter words?

   AR ( )
   ER ( )
   BA ( )
   TE ( )
   AI ( )
   BA ( )

4. What is the total of the numbers on the reverse side of these dice?

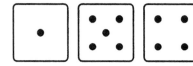

   (a) 18
   (b) 19
   (c) 20
   (d) 21
   (e) 22

5. Insert the letters into the blanks to complete two words which mean the same as the words above them.

BCCEEEGILNORRSUU

SOMBER   REPETITION

- - - U - R - - - -   - - - U - R - - - -

6. Place a word in the brackets that means the same as the two words on either side of the brackets.

penalty (. . . .) excellent

7. When the plan is folded to form a cube, just one of the following can be produced. Which one?

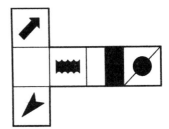

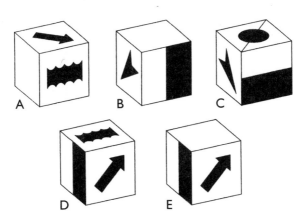

8. Find the two words that are closest in meaning:

juvenile, urchin, bumpkin, waif, minion, malefactor

9. FORTE is to MÉTIER as

INGENUITY is to tact, finesse, prowess, aptitude, artifice

10. Solve this nine-letter-word anagram:

GOOD LINER

11.

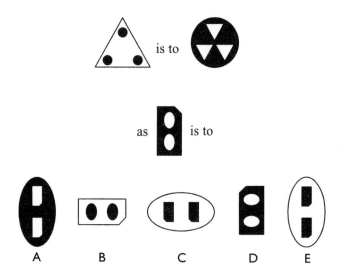

12. What word in the brackets is opposite in meaning to the word in capital letters?

WOODEN (saline, flexible, clear, alert, definite)

13. What word, when placed in the brackets, completes the first word and starts the second word?

RAM (. . . .) ANT

14. HIPPOPHOBIA is to HORSES as

GALEOPHOBIA is to cats, worms, bees, snakes, sharks

15. What number comes next in this sequence?

74823, 22446, 13464, ?

16. What word in the brackets is opposite in meaning to the word in capital letters?

OPTIMUM (glum, minimal, mandatory, distant, close)

17. What four-letter word can be added to each pair of letters to form three new words?

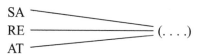

18. Find the item below that is always a part of:

PRALINE

cherries, nuts, licorice, strawberries, marzipan

19. Which word means the same as the one in capital letters?

KNOLL

hillock, knot, skull, gnarled, ravine

20. What is a hogshead? Is it:

    (a) a pig
    (b) a bone
    (c) a cask
    (d) a cannon
    (e) a boar

21. Insert a word that completes the first word and starts the second word.

    short (. . . .) gap

22.

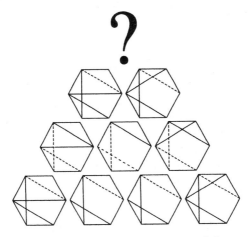

Which hexagon is missing from the top of the pyramid?

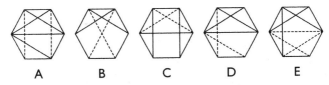

   A   B   C   D   E

23. Which option below is missing from the bottom right-hand corner?

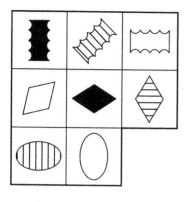

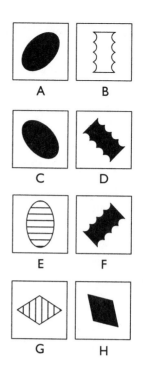

24. Which word can be placed in front to make four new words?

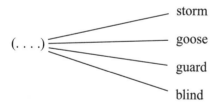

(. . . .) — storm

goose

guard

blind

25. Solve the anagram (one word).
MADE SURE

26. Place 2 three-letter bits together to make a jewel.
NET   CON   ZIR   JEW   GAN   ELY

27. Find the two words that are closest in meaning:
advocate, council, reckon, conclave, endow, mirror

28. Which is the odd one out?
clarion, forint, piccolo, ukulele, zither

29. Which is the missing tile?

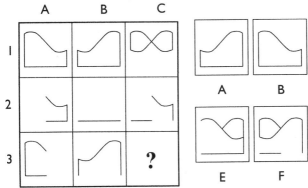

30. Which number comes next in this series?

3 - 7 - 16 - 32 - 57 - ?

31. What creature should go in the brackets reading downward so as to convert the letters to the left of the brackets into three-letter words?

OA ( )
SE ( )
AL ( )
TI ( )
TO ( )
RA ( )

32. Which two words are opposite in meaning?

serious, ill, idle, capricious, still, thin

33. Which option comes next in this sequence?

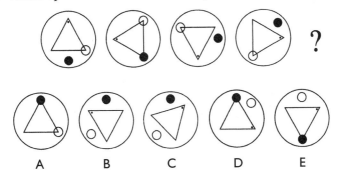

34. Which one of the following is not something you can wear?

DROTALE
WEARSET
MYIHNCE
RUFMOIN
MYSHKAA

35. Insert the word that means the same as the definitions outside the brackets.

iris (. . . .) droop

36. Place 3 two-letter bits together to equal a pet.

PU PD KH OG LA OW

37.

Which option below continues the above sequence?

A   B   C   D   E

38. Which of the following is not a person?

bucolic, jaconet, ascetic, orator, savant

39. What is the area of the graphed shapes?

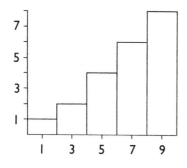

(a) 40
(b) 42
(c) 44
(d) 46
(e) 48

40. Each of the nine squares in the grid marked 1A to 3C should incorporate all the lines and symbols which are shown in the squares of the same letter and number at the top of the column and to the far left. For example, 2B should incorporate all the lines and symbols that are in 2 and B. One of the squares is incorrect. Which one is it?

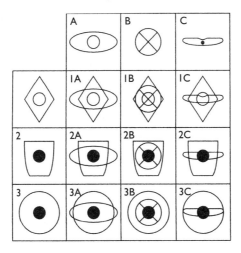

Test One *Answers*

1. C. The rest are the same figure rotated.

2. (a) feint   (b) faint

3. CANARY: to form arc, era, ban, tea, air and bay.

4. (c) 20: Number plus reverse always equals 7
so $6 + 2 + 3 + 4 + 5 = 20$

5. lugubrious, recurrence

6. fine

7. A.

8. urchin, waif

9. artifice

10. gondolier

11. E. The rectangle with the corner missing flips over and two of them go inside the ellipse in the same position that the ellipses had previously been in inside the rectangle. The ellipse remains white and the rectangle remains black.

12. flexible

13. PAGE: to make rampage and pageant.

14. sharks: hippophobia is fear of horses, galeophobia is fear of sharks.

15. 5384 $7482 \times 3 = 22446$
$2244 \times 6 = 13464$
$1346 \times 4 = 5384$

16. minimal

17. TIRE: to make satire, retire, attire.

18. nuts

19. hillock

20. (c) a cask

21. stop

22. D. The contents of each hexagon are determined by the contents of the two hexagons below it. The contents are merged in the following way. Where just one line appears, either dotted or complete it is carried forward. Where two complete lines appear in the same position they are carried forward but become dotted. Where two dotted lines appear in the same position they are carried forward but become complete.

23. A. So that in each line across and down there is an upright, diagonal and horizontal figure and a black, striped and white figure. Horizontal lines contain the same figure and vertical lines contain one each of the three different figures.

24. snow

25. measured

26. zircon

27. council, conclave

28. forint: a monetary unit, the others are musical instruments.

29. E.
Col. A + Col. B = Col. C
Line 1 + Line 2 = Line 3
But similar parts of symbols disappear.

30. 93 (differences: 2^2, 3^2, 4^2, 5^2, 6^2)

31. FALCON: to produce oaf, sea, all, tic, too, and ran.

32. capricious, serious

33. A.
Triangle revolves 90 degrees counterclockwise
● revolves 45 degrees counterclockwise
○ revolves 90 degrees counterclockwise

34. MYIHNCE = CHIMNEY. The items which can be worn are leotard, sweater, uniform and yashmak.

35. flag

36. lapdog

37. C. The diamond rotates counterclockwise pointing at each corner (or pair of corners) in turn at each stage. The line rotates clockwise pointing at middle of line, corner, middle of line in turn.

38. jaconet: a cotton fabric.

39. (b)
$42 = (21 \times 2) = (1 \times 2) + (2 \times 2) + (4 \times 2) + (6 \times 2) + (8 \times 2)$

40. 1C

Test Two

1.

Which option below continues the above sequence?

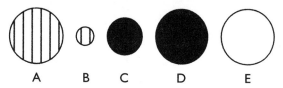

    A   B   C   D   E

2. Consider the following list of words:

KNOT, GLOW, FORT, HINT, BEST

Now choose just one of the following words which you think has something in common with them:

NAVY, DIRT, PART, TALK, TRAP, PITY

3. A number of antonyms of the keyword are shown. Take one letter from each of the antonyms to find a further antonym of the keyword. The letters appear in the correct order.

Keyword: FRANK

Antonyms: INDIRECT, UNDERHANDED, ARTFUL, SHIFTY, RETICENT, SHY

4. Which is the odd one out?

cornea, pupil, lobe, iris, lens

5. What number comes next in this sequence?

123, 117, 108, 99, ?

6. Solve this nine-letter-word anagram:

CHANT PERM

7.

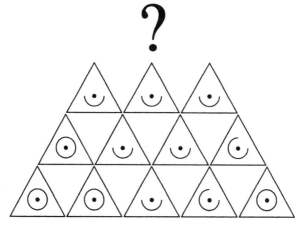

Which set of triangles is missing from the top of the pyramid?

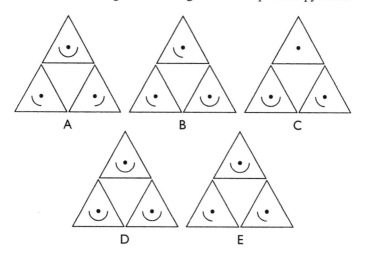

8. Which one of these is not a color shade?

TROPCIA   *Apricot*
SMORBEA
MEARNIC
SCRNOIM   *crimson*
TSERALC   *scarlet*

9. IDEAL is to PRINCIPLE as
IDIOM is to moron, deity, torpor, parlance, token

10. Which of the five squares on the right has most in common with the square on the left?

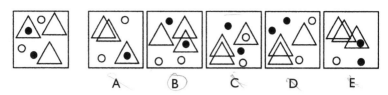

A B C D E

11. ABCDEFGH

What letter is immediately to the right of the letter, two to the right of the letter immediately to the left of the letter three to the right of the letter C?

12. What creature is missing from the brackets?

NUT(PIG)SKIN
TROT(?)HOLE

13. What word in the brackets is opposite in meaning to the word in capital letters?

OPULENT (bleak, destitute, gentle, thin, uniform)

14. What number should replace the question mark?

36		23	17		14	58		46
	3			2			?	
47		28	26		11	98		45

15. Which is the odd one out?

rabbi, shaman, nuncio, dean, insurgent

16. Find the item below that is always a part of:

CURACAO
milk, lemon, orange, coffee, ginger

17. Which domino is next in this sequence?

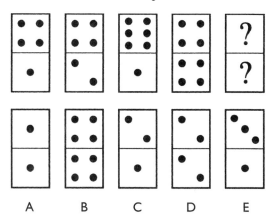

A   B   C   D   E

18. Which of the following is not a weapon?

blunderbuss, bastinado, stiletto, knobkerrie, hector

19. Insert the word that means the same as the definitions outside the brackets.

desert (. . . .) brownish crimson

20. Solve the anagram (one word).

NINE PUGS

21.

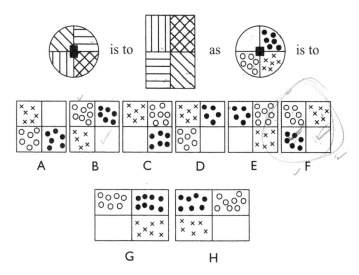

22. Which of the following pieces forms a perfect square when fitted to the piece opposite?

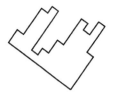

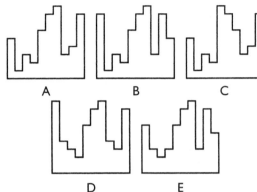

23. Insert a word which completes the first word and starts the second word.

slide (. . . .) book

24. Find the word which means the same as

TERMAGENT

beetle, virgin, sow, virago, witch

25. Which two words are opposite in meaning?

colossal, freedom, vassalage, delicate, taut, helical

26.

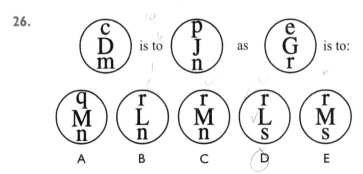

27.

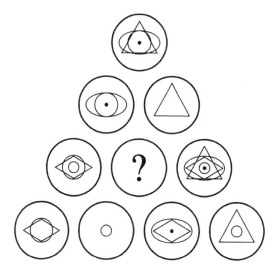

Which circle below fits into the center circle to complete the sequence?

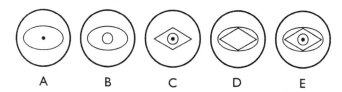

A B C D E

28. What word in the brackets means the same as the word in capital letters?

ABORIGINAL (basic, Australian, primeval, opposite, nomadic)

29. Which is the odd one out?

dors-, fore-, noto-, retro-, ana-

30. What word is missing from the brackets?

OWL (LEAD) INVADE
RAG (. . . .) BEWARE

31. Place 3 two-letter bits together to equal a loose robe.

NO GO MO WN WI KI

32. Which shape should be placed at ?

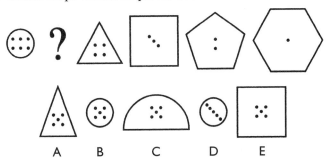

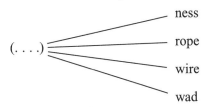

| A | B | C | D | E |

33.
A	E	J
D	?	M
H	L	Q

What letter should replace the question mark?

34. Which word can be placed in front to make four new words?

(. . . .)
- ness
- rope
- wire
- wad

35.

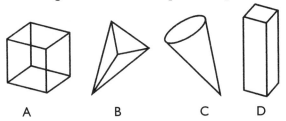

Which figure below should replace the question mark?

| A | B | C | D |

36. If the die is rolled one face to square 2, and so on one face at a time to 3-4-5-6, which number will appear on the top face on square 6?

  (a) 1
  (b) 2
  (c) 3
  (d) 4
  (e) 5
  (f) 6

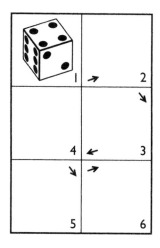

37. Which number comes next in the series?

5, 6, 8, 4, 12, 1, 17, ?

38. What is the name given to a group of eagles? Is it:

  (a) a flight
  (b) a dip
  (c) a swoop
  (d) a stealth
  (e) a convocation

39.

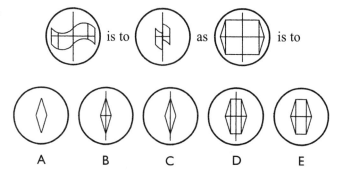

40. Each of the nine squares in the grid marked 1A to 3C should incorporate all the lines and symbols which are shown in the squares of the same letter and number immediately above and to the left. For example, 2B should incorporate all the lines and symbols that are in 2 and B. One of the squares is incorrect. Which one is it?

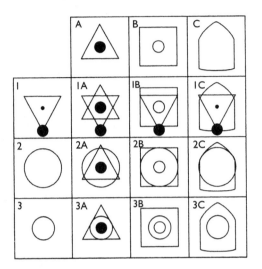

Test Two *Answers*

1. D. There are three sizes of circles rising from small to large, then descending large to small in turn. The circles are black, white, striped in turn.

2. DIRT: all the words have their letters in alphabetical order.

3. crafty

4. lobe: it is part of the ear, the rest are parts of the eye.

5. 81:
$123-6 (1 + 2 + 3) = 117,$
$117-9 (1 + 1 + 7) = 108,$
$108-9 (1 + 0 + 8) = 99,$
$99-18 (9 + 9) = 81$

6. parchment

7. D. The dot is carried forward always; however, only parts of the circle common to both triangles below are carried forward to the triangle above.

8. SMORBEA = AMBROSE. The color shades are apricot, carmine, crimson and scarlet.

9. parlance

10. B: it contains three triangles, two black dots and two white dots, and one of the black dots is in a triangle.

11. H

12. FOX: to make fox-trot and foxhole.

13. destitute

14. 4:
$47 - 23 = 24, \quad 36 - 28 = 8, \quad 24 \div 8 = 3$
$26 - 14 = 12, \quad 17 - 11 = 6, \quad 12 \div 6 = 2$
$98 - 46 = 52, \quad 58 - 45 = 13, \quad 52 \div 13 = 4$

15. insurgent: the others are all officials.

16. orange

17. C. There are two sequences:

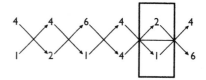

18. hector

19. maroon

20. penguins

21. F. The segments in the circle transfer to the square in the middle as follows:
top left goes to bottom right, top right goes to bottom left, bottom left goes to top left, and bottom right goes to top right.

22. A.

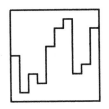

23. rule

24. virago

25. freedom, vassalage

26. E. Top letter advances 13 letters, middle letter advances 6 letters, lower letter advances 1 letter.

27. E. Each circle is produced by joining together the two circles underneath, but similar symbols disappear.

28. primeval

29. fore-: a prefix meaning before, the others meaning back.

30. GEAR: $\underset{1}{\text{OWL}}$ $\underset{1\,2\,3\,4}{\text{(LEAD)}}$ $\underset{3\,4\,2}{\text{INVADE}}$

$\quad\quad\quad\underset{1}{\text{RAG}}$ $\underset{1\,2\,3\,4}{\text{(GEAR)}}$ $\underset{3\,4\,2}{\text{BEWARE}}$

31. kimono

32. (c) Each shape is made up of 1 - 2 - 3 - 4 - 5 - 6 lines. Dots are 6 - 5 - 4 - 3 - 2 - 1.

33. H; running down each line jump 2, then 3, letters. Looking across jump 3, then 4.

34. tight

35. C: the number of surfaces increase by one each time starting with a sphere (one surface). The cone (option C) has two surfaces.

36. (e) 5

37. –3 There are two series:
5, 8, 12, 17 (+ 3, + 4, + 5)
6, 4, 1, –3 (–2, –3, –4)

38. (e) a convocation

39. B. The inner shape contracts into the vertical line on either side.

40. 1B.

Test Three

1. Which is the odd one out?

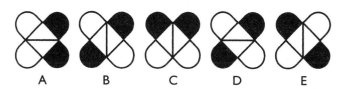

A   B   C   D   E

2. A number of synonyms of the keyword are shown. Take one letter from each of the synonyms to find a further synonym of the keyword. The letters appear in the correct order.

Keyword: MOTIVATE

Synonyms: INSPIRE, INSPIRIT, DRIVE, AROUSE, ACTUATE, PERSUADE

3. STAR is to STELLATE as
   HEART is to capitate, cordate, cultrate, cruciate, clavate

4. What word, when placed in the brackets, completes the first word and starts the second word?
   WAY (. . .) ABOUT

5. Insert the letters into the blanks to complete two words which mean the same as the words above them.

AACEGILNNOPRV

RED   OPERATION
- - - M - - I - -   - - M - - I - -

6. MULTIPLY is to PRODUCT as
   DIVIDE is to number, denominator, factorial, quotient, numerator

7. Place a word in the brackets that means the same as the definitions on either side of the brackets.
   promise (. . . .) state of distress

8.

Which shield is missing from the bottom right-hand corner?

A   B   C   D   E

9. What number should replace the question mark?

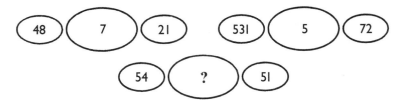

10. Rearrange the letters in the phrase below to spell out three colors.

NOW URGE ON RABBLE

11. Solve this nine-letter-word anagram:

GREY SNOUT

12. SPUR is to RIDGE as

ESCARPMENT is to range, slope, peak, rock, pass

---

13. What four-letter word can be added to each of these letters to form six new words?

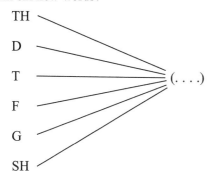

TH
D
T (. . . .)
F
G
SH

14. Find the two words that are closest in meaning:

halt, abolish, change, expunge, reject, detest

15. Find two words which are antonyms. One word reads either clockwise or counterclockwise round the outer circle and the other reads in the opposite direction in the inner circle. You must provide the missing letters.

16. What written number comes next in this sequence?

ONE, FOUR, EIGHT, THIRTEEN, TWENTY ONE, ?

17. What creature is missing from the brackets?

a light grayish brown color (. . . .) court favor servilely

18.

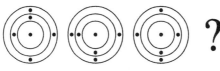

Which option below continues the above sequence?

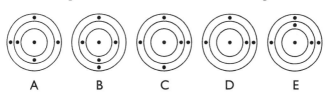

A   B   C   D   E

19. Which four of the pieces below can be fitted together to form a perfect square?

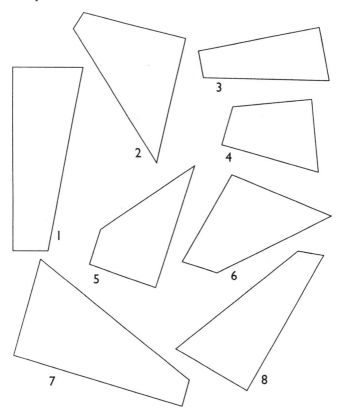

20. Which two words are closest in meaning?

fountain, bed, aquarium, coterie, doves, clique

21. Insert a word which completes the first word and starts the second word.

cave (. . .) kind

22. Find the word which means the same as

RUBICUND

rialto, band, golden, florid, sparkling

23. Place 3 two-letter bits together to equal extinguish.

CH PI EN GA TO QU

24.

Which option below continues the above sequence?

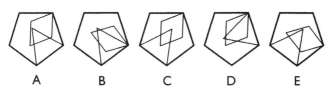

| A | B | C | D | E |

25. Find the item below that is always a part of:
FIANCHETTO
pawn, queen, knight, rook, king

26. What comes next in this series?
6, –9, 13½, –20¼, ?

27. Which of these is not a building term?
mullion, vault, atrium, gazebo, batik

28. Which is the odd one out?
phaeton, landau, sulky, rickshaw, trimaran

29. Insert the word that means the same as the definitions outside the brackets.

harbor bar (. . . .) hollow roar

30.

Which option below should logically follow in this sequence?

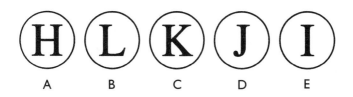

| A | B | C | D | E |

31. The letters of the words CONFIDANT have been set out at right. Starting at the arrow and moving circle to circle, which must be touching circles, moving upward and across left to right, in how many ways can you spell out CONFIDANT?

(a) 7
(b) 8
(c) 9
(d) 10
(e) 11

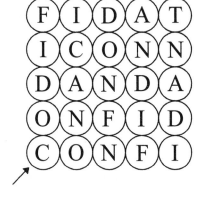

32. Each line and symbol which appears in the four outer circles, at right, is transferred to the center circle according to the following rules:

if a line or symbol occurs in the outer circles:

once: it is transferred
twice: it is possibly transferred
3 times: it is transferred
4 times: it is not transferred.

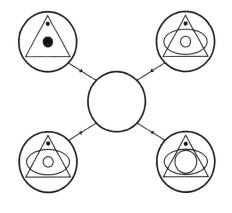

Which of the circles shown below should appear at the center of the diagram above?

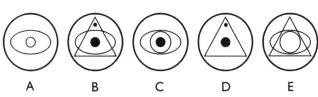

A   B   C   D   E

33. What is a marquee? Is it:

    (a) a grandee

    (b) a count

    (c) a coin

    (d) a canopy

    (e) a duke

34. A number of synonyms of the keyword are shown. Take one letter from each of the synonyms to find a further synonym of the keyword. The letters appear in the correct order.

Keyword: ENDLESS

Synonyms: CEASELESS, UNBOUNDED, ETERNAL, PERPETUAL, UNENDING, INCESSANT, UNLIMITED, CONSTANT, INTERMINABLE

35.

On which two targets has 245 been scored?

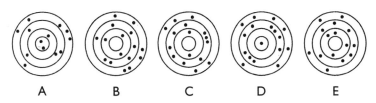

A   B   C   D   E

36. Which two words are opposite in meaning?

wholesome, obfuscate, enlighten, melodramatic, articulate, brief

37. Which word can be placed in front to make four new words?

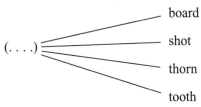

board

shot

thorn

tooth

(. . . .)

38. Solve the anagram (one word).

IRON COPS

39. Place 2 three-letter bits together to equal firepower.

FIR   TER   VOS   INT   SAL   SHO

40.

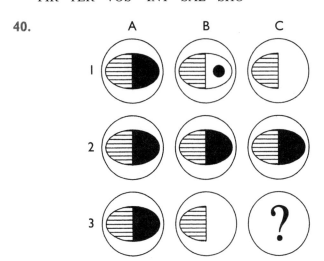

Logically, which option below fits into the blank circle to carry on the pattern?

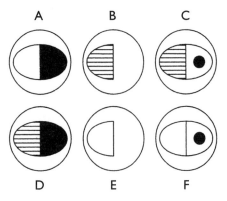

Test Three *Answers*

1. B. A is the same figure as C rotated. D is the same figure as E rotated.

2. INDUCE

3. cordate: stellate is star-shaped, cordate is heart-shaped.

4. LAY: to make waylay and layabout.

5. vermilion, campaign

6. quotient

7. plight

8. C. Looking across and down, the contents of the third shield are determined by the contents of the first two shields. Where a suit appears just once it is simply carried forward. If, however, it appears twice it is carried forward but is turned 180 degrees. (Note that when the diamond rotates 180 degrees it appears the same.)

9. 3. Reverse the numbers in the small ellipses:
$84 \div 12 = 7$, $135 \div 27 = 5$, $45 \div 15 = 3$

10. BROWN, ORANGE, BLUE

11. youngster

12. slope

13. RILL: to make thrill, drill, trill, frill, grill, shrill.

14. abolish, expunge

15. escalate, diminish

16. THIRTY. Add the number of letters in the previous spelled out number each time.
TWENTY ONE has 9 letters, therefore $21 + 9 = $ THIRTY.

17. fawn

18. E. The dots in the outer circle move 90 degrees clockwise each stage, the dots in the middle circle move 90 degrees counter-clockwise each stage, and the dot in the center circle always stays in the center.

19.

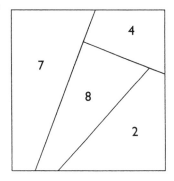

20. coterie, clique

21. man

22. florid

23. quench

24. A. The diamond moves to each corner of the pentagon in turn clockwise. The triangle moves to each side of the pentagon in turn counterclockwise.

25. pawn

26. 30⅜ (multiply by –1½ each time)

27. batik: printed designs on fabric

28. trimaran: the rest are all land vehicles.

29. boom

30. E. LETTER I
W V U T S **R** Q P O N M L K J **I**

31. (c) 9

32. C.

33. (d) a canopy

34. continual

35. A. and E.

36. obfuscate, enlighten

37. buck

38. scorpion

39. salvos

40. B.
Col. A + Col. B = Col. C
Line 1 + Line 2 = Line 3
Only similar parts are carried forward.

Test Four

1. Which option below is missing from the bottom right-hand corner?

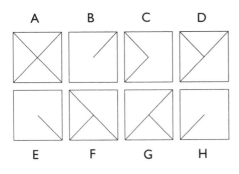

A   B   C   D

E   F   G   H

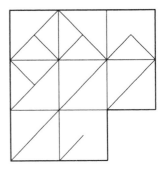

2. BITTER SWEET is to OXYMORON as
   REVERSE BACKWARDS is to simile, metonymy, tautology, syllepsis, hyperbole

3. Find the two words that are opposite in meaning:
   corruption, recrimination, redemption, alienation, rectitude, theft

4. Find two words which are antonyms. One word reads either clockwise or counterclockwise round the outer circle and the other reads in the opposite direction in the inner circle. You must provide the missing letters.

5. Solve this nine-letter-word anagram:
   TOURED FIT

6. MINDFUL is to HEEDLESS as
   MISERLY is to prodigal, parsimonious, happy, fortunate, destitute

7. What word is missing from the brackets?
   TIMEOUS (START) PRIMATE
   NURSING (. . . . .) PANDORA

8.

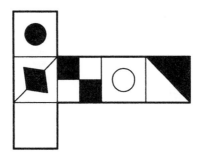

When the above is folded to form a cube, just one of the following can be produced. Which one?

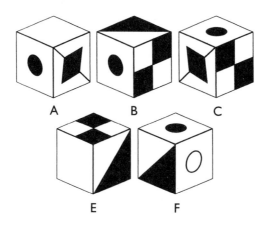

A   B   C

E   F

9. Which word in the brackets means the same as the word in capital letters?

FRATERNIZE (eschew, distract, swindle, concur, purge)

10. TENDER, DIRECT, RANGE, CREDIT, RENTED
Which word below is missing from the above list?
TRAIN, ANGER, DETECT, GREEN, FINAL

11. NE PLUS ULTRA is to PERFECTION as
SUI GENERIS is to indefinitely, charitable, intrinsically, amazing, unique

12. DENSIMETER is to DENSITY as
PLUVIOMETER is to surface area, rainfall, humidity, precise time, intensity

13.

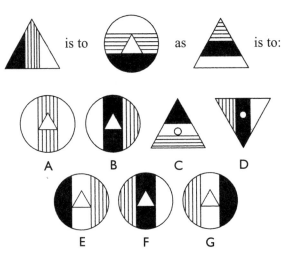

14. Place a word in the brackets that means the same as the definitions on either side of the brackets.

thin sheet metal (. . . .) repulse

15. Which word in the brackets means the same as the word in capital letters?

GREGARIOUS (reserved, hungry, generous, affable, ferocious)

16. MELLOW, VERGE, EASY, MANNER, JUST, SALUTE

What word below continues the above sequence?

SEAT, URBAN, PLEASE, UPRIGHT, OBSERVE

17. What word, when placed in the brackets, completes the first word and starts the second word?

FEAT (. . . .) ON

18. What number is missing from the bottom right-hand corner?

2	4	6	10
5	1	6	7
7	5	12	17
12	6	18	?

19.

Which of the following pieces forms a perfect square when fitted to the above piece?

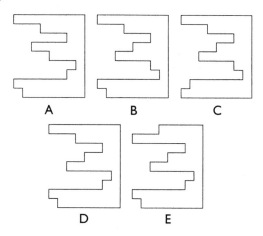

20. What is patois? Is it:

    (a) a patio

    (b) lies

    (c) gangsters

    (d) a dialect

    (e) brothers

21. Solve the anagram (one word).

    ACUTE CALL

22.

Which option below continues the above sequence?

23. Which word can be placed in front to make four new words?

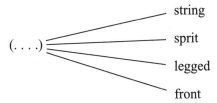

string

sprit

legged

front

24. Which of these is not a dance?

morris, pavane, ramekin, mazurka, farandole

25. Insert the word that means the same as the definitions outside the brackets.

dashing fellow (. . . .) leaf of grass

26.

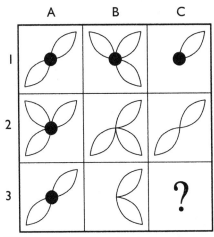

Which of the following is the missing tile?

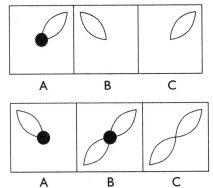

27. Which number should be placed in the center circle?

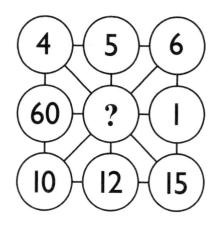

  (a) 15
  (b) 20
  (c) 30
  (d) 45
  (e) 60

28. What is the name given to a group of arrows? Is it:
  (a) a feather
  (b) a bunch
  (c) a quiver
  (d) a point
  (e) a bow

29. Find the word which means the same as
  LEXICON
  parchment, chair, writing desk, dictionary, diary

30. Which is the odd one out?
  mullet, smolt, albatross, gudgeon, grayling

31. Insert a word which completes the first word and starts the second.
  fountain (. . . .) pal

32. Place 2 three-letter bits together to equal a winter sport.
  PIS SKI LOM RUM SLA TEN

33. Which two words are opposite in meaning?
  obese, noxious, similar, verbose, harmless, generous

34. Which two words are closest in meaning?
  basalt, idol, imbecile, hoyden, tomboy, dwarf

35.

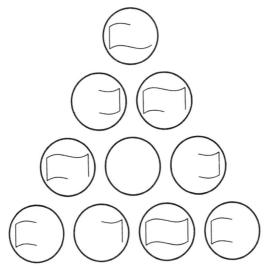

Which of the options below fits into the blank circle above?

A   B   C   D   E

36. Place 3 two-letter bits together to equal a body organ.

TO SP CA EN PU LE

37. Find the item below that is always a part of:

ZABAGLIONE

cheese, sardines, egg yolk, peppers, tomatoes

38. Logically, what number should be inserted to complete the sequence?

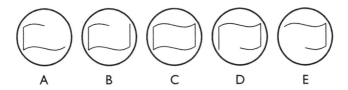

39. What comes next here?

5, 9, 7, 6, 11, 0, 19, ?, ?

40. Which of these is the odd one out?

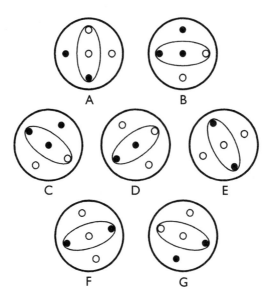

Test Four *Answers*

I. H. The contents of the third square, looking across and down, are determined by the contents of the first two squares. Only lines which appear in both the first two squares are carried forward to the third squares. Lines that only appear once do not appear in the third square.

2. tautology

3. corruption, rectitude

4. official, informal

5. fortitude

6. prodigal

7. GROAN

```
1       2   234 5 1   5    4 3
TIMEOUS (START) PRIMATE
1       2   234 5 1   5    4 3
NURSING (GROAN) PANDORA
```

8. C.

9. concur

10. ANGER: tender and rented, direct and credit, anger and range are anagram pairs.

I I. unique

12. rainfall

13. F. The figure flips 90 degrees left. The triangle turns into a circle and the triangle goes in the center of the circle.

14. foil

15. affable

16. URBAN: The first two letters of each word are the same two letters as the planets in order from the sun: Mercury, Venus, Earth, Mars, Jupiter, Saturn, Uranus.

17. HER: to produce feather and heron.

18. 24. Looking across and down every third number is the sum of the previous two numbers:

$2 + 4 = 6, 4 + 6 = 10$ etc.

19. D.

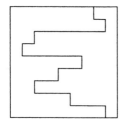

20. (d) a dialect

21. calculate

22. B. The outer curve moves 90 degrees clockwise at each stage, the inner curve moves 90 degrees counterclockwise at each stage and the center curve moves 90 degrees clockwise at each stage.

23. bow

24. ramekin: a baked dish.

25. blade

26. C.
Col. A + Col. B = Col. C
Line 1 + Line 2 = Line 3
Only similar parts are carried forward.

27. (e) 60
4 × 15 = 60, 5 × 12 = 60,
6 × 10 = 60, 60 × 1 = 60.

28. (c) a quiver

29. dictionary

30. albatross: the rest are all fish.

31. pen

32. slalom

33. noxious, harmless

34. hoyden, tomboy

35. A. Each circle is produced by combining the parts in the two circles below, but similar parts disappear.

36. spleen

37. egg yolk

38. 24.

$$\frac{6 \times 4 \times 8}{3 \times 2 \times 2} = 16$$

$$\frac{3 \times 14 \times 2}{1 \times 7 \times 2} = 6$$

$$\frac{6 \times 18 \times 8}{2 \times 4 \times 9} = 12$$

$$\frac{12 \times 4 \times 18}{9 \times 4 \times 3} = 8$$

$$\frac{6 \times 10 \times 12}{3 \times 2 \times 5} = 24$$

39. −12. There are two series:
5, 7, 11, 19 (+2, +4, +8)
9, 6, 0, −12 (−3, −6, −12)

40. D. A is the same as G, B is the same as C, E is the same as F.

Test Five

1. Which option below is missing from the bottom right-hand corner?

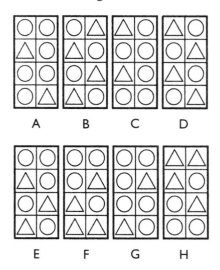

A   B   C   D

E   F   G   H

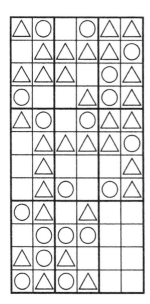

2. Fill in the missing word:

DOME (MODERATE) TEAR

NEST (. . . .) LINE

3. Solve this nine-letter-word anagram:

SUIT PLATE

4. What word in the brackets is opposite in meaning to the word in capital letters?

IRRATIONAL (suitable, decisive, logical, careful, smooth)

5. Find two words which are antonyms. One word reads either clockwise or counterclockwise round the outer circle and the other reads in the opposite direction in the inner circle. You must provide the missing letters.

6. What four-letter word can be added to each of these letters to form five new words?

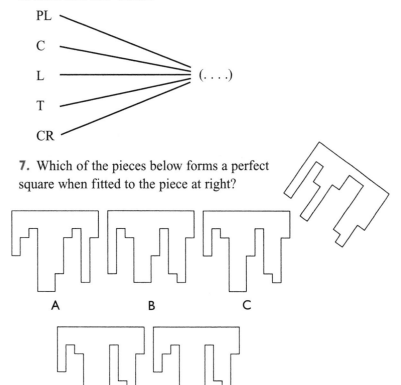

PL
C
L
T
CR
(. . . .)

7. Which of the pieces below forms a perfect square when fitted to the piece at right?

A   B   C

D   E

8. OVERUSED is to CLICHÉD as
OVERATTENTIVE is to chintzy, scholastic, irritable, imperious, officious

9. Find the two words that are closest in meaning:
remove, espouse, erudite, shallow, accurate, knowledgeable

10. What word, when placed in the brackets, completes the first word and starts the second word?

CAP (. . .) RENT

---

11. Which shield at right is missing from the bottom right-hand corner?

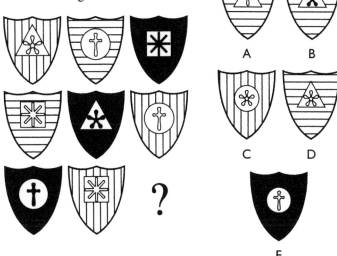

A B C D

E

12. A B C D E F G H
What letter is two to the left of the letter immediately to the left of the letter four to the right of the letter immediately to the right of the letter C?

13. Which one of these is not a form of transport?

CRTAORT
TROCAHI
ANRVCAA
DRLEEMA
SNOMBUI

14. Find the two words that are closest in meaning:

maudlin, worried, sad, slow, angry, tearful

15. HUMANE is to RUTHLESS as

HUMBLE is to obsequious, interesting, facetious, pretentious, deferential

16. Solve this nine-letter-word anagram:

I MADE TIME

17.

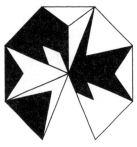

Which section is missing from the above octagon?

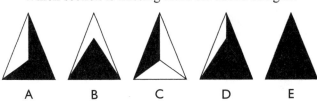

| A | B | C | D | E |

18. What word in the brackets is opposite in meaning to the word in capital letters?

SOMBER (busy, engrossed, funny, garish, composed)

19. Find the two words that are opposite in meaning:

eternal, nonstop, unique, punctuated, noteworthy, lucid

20. Find the item below that is always a part of:

POMANDER

flour, eggs, fragrance, salt, pepper

21. Find the word that means the same as:

CAPRICE

meaning, dish, fancy, dance, hat

22. Insert a word which completes the first word and starts the second word.

movie (. . . .) off

23. Which is the odd one out?

shoveler, whimbrel, cassowary, ptarmigan, dace

24. Place 3 two-letter bits together to equal a mountain range.

RA   DA   PI   ER   SI   TO

25. Which two words are closest in meaning?

brilliance, escarpment, eclat, meeting, trade, compound

26. Which word can be placed in front to make four new words?

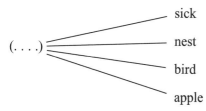

(. . . .) sick nest bird apple

27.

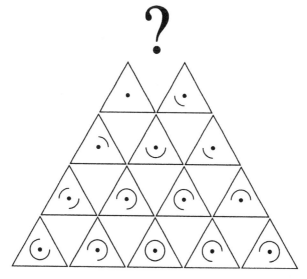

What triangle is missing from the top of the pyramid?

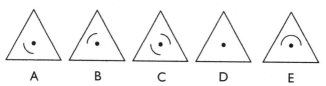

A   B   C   D   E

28.

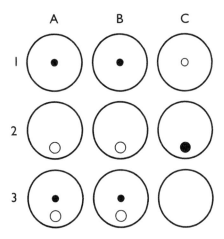

Logically, which of the options below fits into the blank circle to carry on the pattern?

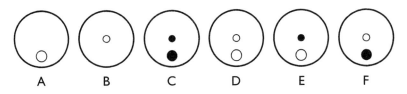

29. Solve the anagram (one word).

FORMALIN

30. What is a sepoy? Is it:

(a) a cabbage
(b) a soldier
(c) pasta
(d) a vehicle
(e) a jar

31. Insert the word that means the same as the definitions outside the brackets.

small sphere (. . . .) building material

32. Which two words are opposite in meaning?

glossary, schism, patriarch, parody, union, schematic

33.

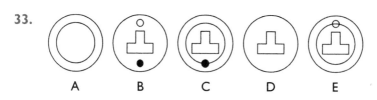

A   B   C   D   E

Which of the options above fits into the middle circle to carry on a logical sequence?

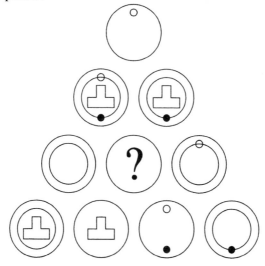

34. Which number comes next in this series?

7, 21, 84, 420, ?

35. What is the name given to a group of scouts? Is it:

(a) a bevy
(b) a chattering
(c) a dissimilation
(d) a service
(e) a jamboree

36. Place 2 three-letter bits together to equal an animal.

PIG   RIN   GOP   RUN   LAT   HER

37. Which of these is not an aquatic creature?

mantis, grampus, lamprey, albacore, halibut

38.

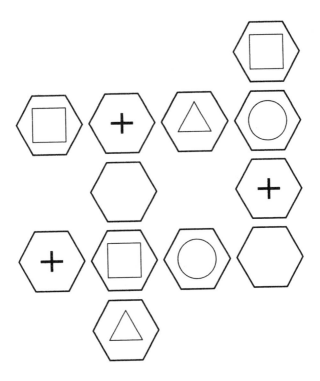

Which two symbols should go into the two blank hexagons?

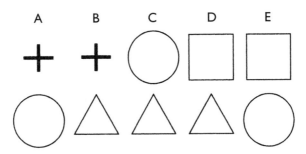

A   B   C   D   E

39.

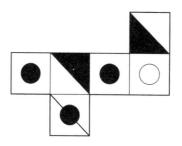

Which of the six cubes shown cannot be constructed from the net of the cube?

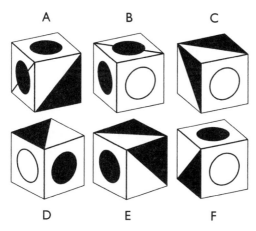

A   B   C

D   E   F

40. How many times will this piece of jigsaw fit into the shape?

   (a) 10
   (b) 11
   (c) 12
   (d) 13
   (e) 14

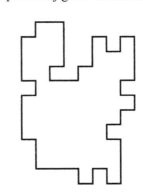

Test Five *Answers*

1. G. The contents of the third rectangle, looking both across and down, are determined by the contents of the previous two rectangles. Where a symbol appears in the same position in both rectangles it changes from a circle to a triangle or vice-versa in the third rectangle. Where a symbol only appears in a position once it is simply carried forward.

2. SENTINEL: NEST is an anagram of SENT and LINE is an anagram of INEL.

3. stipulate

4. logical

5. graceful, ungainly

6. ease: to give please, cease, lease, tease and crease.

7. D.

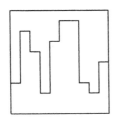

8. officious

9. erudite, knowledgeable

10. tor: to give captor and torrent.

11. D. Each horizontal and vertical line contains each of the three crosses; a triangle, circle and square; a black, horizontal striped and vertical striped background; and just one of the crosses black.

12. E

13. DRLEEMA = EMERALD. The forms of transport are: tractor, chariot, caravan and omnibus.

14. maudlin, tearful

15. pretentious

16. immediate

17. A. Opposite segments are mirror images but with black and white reversed.

18. garish

19. nonstop, punctuated

20. fragrance

21. fancy

22. show

23. dace: a fish, the rest are birds.

24. sierra

25. brilliance, eclat

26. love

27. A. The contents of the second row of triangles are formed by carrying forward parts of the circle common to the two triangles immediately below. The contents of the third row, however, are the uncommon parts of the circles below. The contents of the fourth row revert to common parts and the contents of the top (fifth row) revert to uncommon parts. The central dot is always carried forward.

28. F.
Col. A + Col. B = Col. C
Line 1 + Line 2 = Line 3
Similar circles change color.

29. informal

30. (b) a soldier

31. marble

32. schism, union

33. B. Each circle is produced by combining together the two circles below, but similar symbols disappear.

34. 2520 ($\times$ 3, $\times$ 4, $\times$ 5, $\times$ 6)

35. (e) a jamboree

36. gopher

37. mantis

38. C. Each line of 4 hexagons must contain $\square$, $\triangle$, $\bigcirc$, + in any order.

39. C

40. (c) 12

Test Six

1.

Which option below is missing from the bottom right-hand corner?

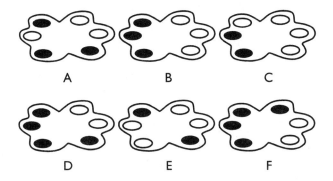

2. Which is the odd one out?

anorak, mantle, kirtle, camisole, burnoose

3. What word, when placed in the brackets, completes the first word and starts the second word?

HUM (. . . .) HEAD

4. What number is missing from the brackets?

961 (43)
1852 (59)
463 (?)

5. Find the two words that are opposite in meaning:

angry, cynical, disappointed, gullible, gregarious, caustic

6. Solve this nine-letter-word anagram:

CREAM TINS

7. Insert the letters into the blanks to complete two words which mean the same as the words above them.

ABEEGNNT

OBVIOUS   TASTEFUL

- L - - A - T   - L - - A - T

8. Place a word in the brackets that means the same as the definitions on either side of the brackets.

a small windlass (. . . .) stagger

9. POST- is to LATER as

MACRO- is to large, last, late, language, small

10.

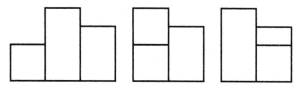

Which option below continues the above sequence?

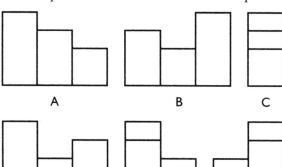

A	B	C
D	E	F

11.

Which option below continues the above sequence?

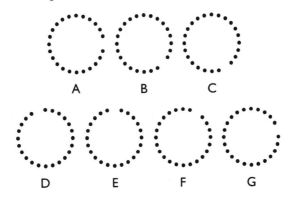

12. Which is the odd one out?

    lancet, bay, rose, oriel, portal

13. Which is the odd one out?

    serenade, eulogize, yodel, croon, warble

14. What word, when placed in the brackets, completes the first word and starts the second word?

    KEY (. . . .) DOCK

15. Consider the following list of words:

    TIDE, NUTS, REED, WARD

Now choose just one of the following words which you think has most in common with them:

    CALM, STAR, TRAY, EVER, WOOL

16. What number is missing from the third pyramid?

17. Which four of the pieces below can be fitted together to form a perfect square?

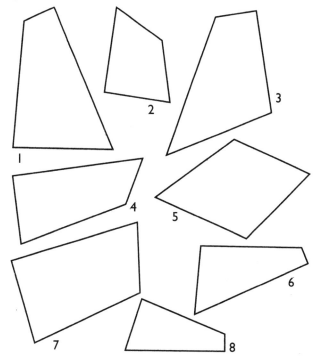

18. What two-letter word is missing from the segment with the question mark?

19. What word in the brackets means the same as the word in capital letters?

KNAVISH (selfish, fraudulent, narrow, canny, cutting)

20. Complete the words, which are synonymous, clockwise or counterclockwise.

21.

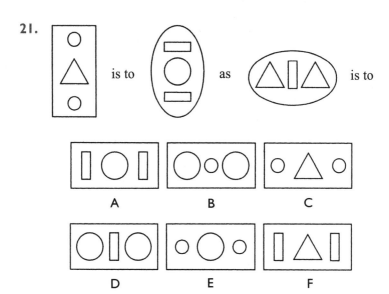

22. Insert a word which completes the first word and starts the second word.

golden (. . . .) gown

23. What is a coulee? Is it:
- (a) a servant
- (b) a ravine
- (c) a boulder
- (d) a waterfall
- (e) a barricade

24. Which word can be placed in front to make four new words?

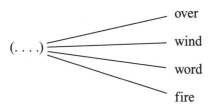

25. Solve the anagram (one word).

A MAN'S RAG

26. How many squares are there in this figure?

  (a) 52
  (b) 53
  (c) 54
  (d) 55
  (e) 56

27. Place 3 two-letter bits together to equal claptrap.

  GE BU LI HA UM NK

28. Find the item below that is always a part of:

JABOT

cardboard, lace, leather, steel mesh, porcelain

29. Find the word that means the same as:

CODDLE

sumac, wrap, swaddle, indulge, cook

30. Insert the word that means the same as the definitions outside the brackets.

  hurl (. . . .) boat

31. What is the name given to a group of stars?

  (a) penumbra
  (b) solstice
  (c) parsec
  (d) galaxy
  (e) magnitude

32. Which two words are opposite in meaning?

hackneyed, thralldom, generosity, liberty, interface, terror

33. Which two words are closest in meaning?

circular, theatre, circus, funicular, railway, arcade

34. Which one of these cannot have its six letters rearranged into a six-letter word?

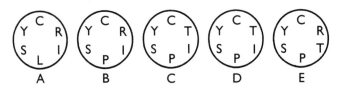

A B C D E

35. Which of these is not a musical instrument?

LUFET

RAHP

ABUT

WETOR

TOCREN

36. Which of these is not a bone?

patella, carpus, tartar, scapula, humerus

37. Which is the odd one out?

shantung, organdy, yashmak, fustian, chamois

38. What is the value of this angle?

(a) 55°
(b) 60°
(c) 65°
(d) 70°
(e) 75°

39.

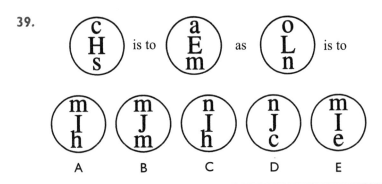

A B C D E

40. Which option fits into the blank circle to carry on a logical sequence?

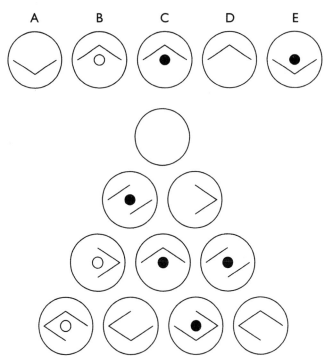

Test Six *Answers*

1. D. Looking along each line and down each column, the contents of the third cloud are determined by the contents of the first two clouds in the following way. Where just one ellipse appears in a certain position it is carried forward to the third cloud. However, where two ellipses appear in the same position they are carried forward, but two white ellipses change to black and vice-versa.

2. camisole: it is an under-garment, the rest are outerwear.

3. drum: to produce humdrum and drumhead.

4. 62. Reverse each number and take the square root of the component parts:
961-169 √16 = 4, √9 = 3 = 43
therefore,
463-364 √36 = 6, √4 = 2 = 62

5. cynical, gullible

6. miscreant

7. blatant, elegant

8. reel

9. large

10. A.
At the first stage the three parts are in the position illustrated. At each subsequent stage the figure (i) moves to the right one position at a time.

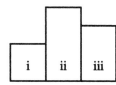

11. B. The gap moves clockwise, first by one dot, then two dots, then three dots, etc.

12. portal: it is a type of door, the rest are types of windows.

13. eulogize: uses the speaking voice, the rest are sung.

14. pad, to produce keypad and paddock.

15. star: they all produce another word when read backwards.

16. 12: $7 \times 8 \div 4 = 14$,
$5 \times 4 \div 2 = 10$,
$18 \times 6 \div 9 = 12$

17.

18. AS. Each two-letter word is produced by the numbers in opposite segments. Take the corresponding letters of the alphabet in respect of their numbered position: A = 1, B = 2, etc. For example: 235 = 23, 5 = WE and 119 = 1, 19 = AS. (The letters produced by 11, 9 = KI do not result in a two-letter word.)

19. fraudulent

20. waxworks, effigies

21. B. The large ellipse becomes a rectangle, the small rectangle becomes a small circle, the triangles become large circles.

22. wedding

23. (b) a ravine

24. cross

25. anagrams

26. (d) 55
(1^2) $1 - 5 \times 5$
(2^2) $4 - 4 \times 4$
(3^2) $9 — 3 \times 3$
(4^2) $16 — 2 \times 2$
(5^2) $25 — 1 \times 1$

27. bunkum

28. lace

29. indulge

30. launch

31. (d) galaxy

32. thralldom, liberty

33. funicular, railway

34. C. The others are lyrics, crispy, script, crypts.

35. WETOR = TOWER. The others are: flute, harp, tuba, cornet.

36. tartar

37. yashmak: the rest are all names of materials.

38. (b) 60°

39. A.   c   b   a
         H   G   F   E
         s r q p o n m

         o   n   m
         L   K   J   I
         n m l k j i h

40. C. Each circle is produced by combining the two lower circles, but similar symbols disappear.

Test Seven

1.

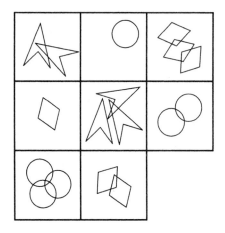

Which option below is missing from the bottom right-hand corner?

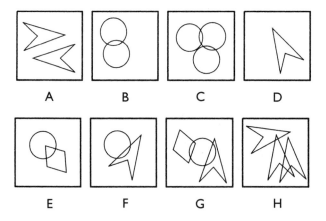

2. Which word in the brackets means the same as the word in capital letters?

PRINCIPLE (majesty, dictum, cost, capital, leader)

3. Solve this nine-letter-word anagram:

DON IN RACE

4. Which word in the brackets is opposite in meaning to the word in capital letters?

ACRIMONIOUS (benign, sharp, churlish, smooth, qualified)

5. WARLOCK is to MALE WITCH as

SHAMAN is to wizard, witch doctor, sorcerer, female vampire, witch-hunter

6. Which four of the pieces below can be fitted together to form a perfect square?

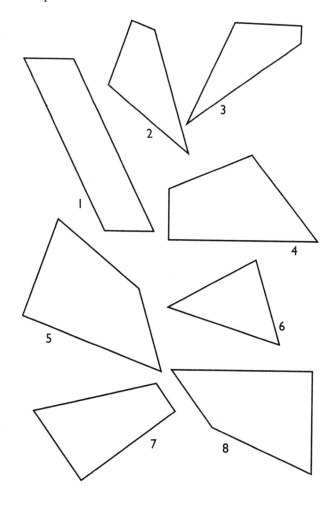

7. Underline the two words that are closest in meaning.

casual, largess, charity, mischief, great, destiny

8. Which of the five boxes on the right has most in common with the box on the left?

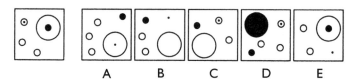

9. Which is the odd one out?

bisque, ebony, jet, sable, raven

10. What word, when placed in the brackets, completes the first word and starts the second word?

HAT (. . . .) DEN

11. What word is missing from the brackets?

BARONET (ROBIN) REBUILD
DREADED (. . . .) TEMPEST

12. Which word in the brackets means the same as the word in capital letters?

VOLUBLE (optional, articulate, ample, epicurean, avid)

13. Underline the two words that are opposite in meaning:

flexible, intrepid, patient, afraid, elated, cheap

14.

Which option below continues the above sequence?

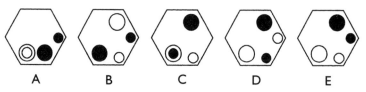

15. What word in the brackets is opposite in meaning to the word in capital letters?

SECULAR (sacred, earthly, exposed, liberal, prime)

16. Which two words that sound alike but are spelled differently mean:

(a) instrument

(b) kind of fine thin silk

17. 2025 is to 45 as

6724 is to 43, 54, 82, 136, or 336

18. A B C D E F G H

What letter is two to the right of the letter three to the left of the letter two to the right of the letter three to the left of the letter H?

19. Find the two words that are closest in meaning:

apply, patronize, fuse, gainsay, revenue, contradict

20. When the above is folded to form a cube, just one of the following can be produced. Which one?

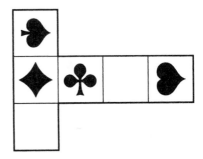

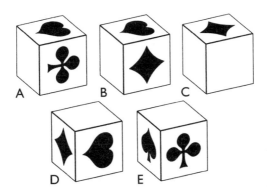

21. Which of these is not a mineral?

gneiss, graphite, puncheon, bauxite, antimony

22. Complete the words which are synonyms, clockwise or counterclockwise.

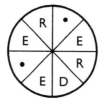 

23. Insert the word that means the same as the definitions outside the brackets.

turban cloth (. . . .) sliding window frame

24. Which is the odd one out?

jacinth, chicane, sardonyx, carbuncle, marcasite

25. Which one of these is not a composer?

LIBZERO
LADIVVI
CINIPUC
SOAPSIC
DOORNIB

26. Which two words are closest in meaning?

cafe, wig, umbrella, gaffe, blunder, pontoon

27. Place 3 two-letter bits together to equal a garment.

RO UD PR AL ES   SH

28. What is a scow? Is it:

(a) a frown
(b) a crane
(c) a game
(d) a bone
(e) a boat

29.

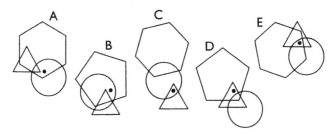

Which of these sets of shapes is most like the example below?

30. Find the item below that is always a part of:

SUCCOTASH

cabbage, corn, butter, bread, honey

31. Insert a word which completes the first word and starts the second word.

swag (. . .) power

32. Which two words are opposite in meaning?

vexatious, vivacious, fixation, satisfying, divided, fanciful

33. In how many different ways can you form the word SPEED from the letters at right, taken in any order?

(a) 18
(b) 20
(c) 22
(d) 24
(e) 26

S	P	P	E
E	S	E	D

34. Find the word that means the same as:

BURLESQUE

caricature, circus, stage, magical, mime

35.

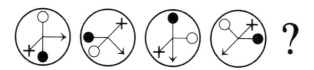

Which option below comes next in this sequence?

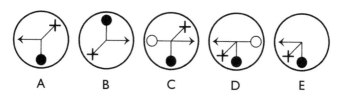

A   B   C   D   E

36. Which word can be placed in front to make four new words?

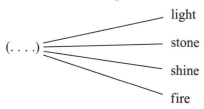

(. . . .)
— light
— stone
— shine
— fire

37. Which one of these is not a boat?

CHUNLA

FIKSF

ONACE

HCAYT

TOBLET

38. Find the two words that are closest in meaning:

case, note, wall, wad, rock, lump

39. A team of 4 gymnasts is to be selected from 4 men and 4 women. How many different teams can be selected if each team must include at least 3 men?

(a) 15

(b) 16

(c) 17

(d) 18

(e) 19

40. Logically, which option fits into the blank circle to carry on the pattern?

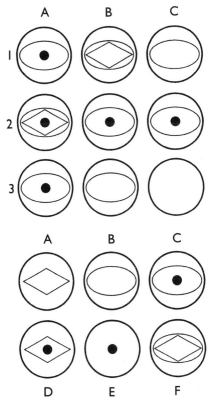

Test Seven *Answers*

1. D. Each horizontal and vertical line contains a box with a different symbol, also a box with one symbol, two symbols and three symbols.

2. dictum

3. ordinance

4. benign

5. witch doctor

6.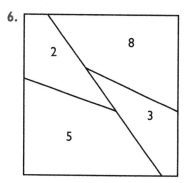

7. largess, charity

8. A. It contains a large circle, three small white circles, a small back circle and a dot.

9. bisque: it is white, the rest are black.

10. red: to produce hatred and redden.

11. TAMED

2 5   1 2 345   1   3   4
BARONET (ROBIN) REBUILD

2 5   1 2 345   1   3   4
DREADED (TAMED) TEMPEST

12. articulate

13. intrepid, afraid

14. E. The large black circle moves backwards and forwards to opposite corners of the hexagon. The large white circle moves round one corner at a time clockwise. The small black circle moves backwards and forwards to opposite corners. The small white circle moves backwards and forwards to opposite corners.

15. sacred

16. tool, tulle

17. 82. It is the square root of 6724. 45 is the square root of 2025.

18. F

19. gainsay, contradict

20. D

21. puncheon

22. deserter, absentee

23. sash

24. chicane: the others are all semi-precious jewels.

25. SOAPSIC = PICASSO. He was an artist. The composers are Berlioz, Vivaldi, Puccini and Borodin.

26. gaffe, blunder

27. shroud

28. (e) a boat

29. E. The dot appears in triangle, circle and hexagon.

30. corn

31. man

32. vexatious, satisfying

33. (d) S2 × P2 × E6 = 24

34. caricature

35. E
━● moves 90 degrees clockwise
━○ moves 135 degrees counterclockwise
━✗ moves 180 degrees
━→ moves 45 degrees clockwise

36. moon

37. TOBLET = BOTTLE. The boats are: launch, skiff, canoe, and yacht.

38. wad, lump

39. (c) 17

(3 men) $\dfrac{4 \times 3 \times 2}{1 \times 2 \times 3} = 4$

(4 men) $\dfrac{1 \times 2 \times 3 \times 4}{1 \times 2 \times 3 \times 4} = 1$

(1 woman) $\dfrac{4}{1} = 4$

Total $4 \times 4 + 1 = 17$

40. B. Col. A + Col. B = Col. C
Line 1 + Line 2 = Line 3
Only similar symbols are carried forward.

Test Eight

1.

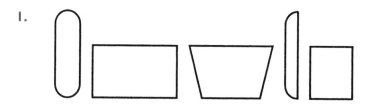

Which option below continues the above sequence?

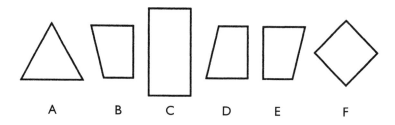

| A | B | C | D | E | F |

2. What word, when placed in the brackets, completes the first word and starts the second word?

TAIL (. . . .) BREAK

3. What word is missing from the brackets?
STIRRED (RIDER) CREEPER
SOUPCON (. . . .) UPRIGHT

4. What word in the brackets means the same as the word in capital letters?

CROOKED (rough, crumpled, ruthless, round, angled)

5. Which one of these is not food?
BMAL
ADREB
TEBRUT
TONCOT
NOCBA

6. A number of antonyms of the keyword are shown. Take one letter from each of the antonyms to find a further antonym of the keyword. The letters appear in the correct order.

Keyword: POLITE

Antonyms: UNCULTURED, IMPERTINENT, DISCOURTEOUS, IMPUDENT, UNREFINED

7.

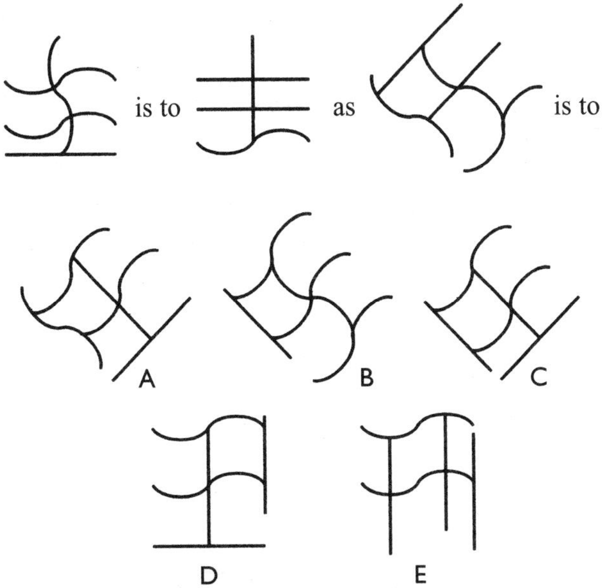

8. Solve this nine-letter-word anagram:

ONCE A WALL

9. What word in the brackets is opposite in meaning to the word in capital letters?

EFFICACIOUS (productive, dull, useless, boring, difficult)

10. Which two words that sound alike but are spelled differently mean:

(a) encroach
(b) spoke violently

11.

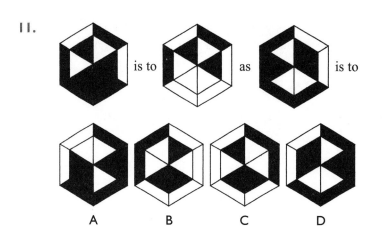

A   B   C   D

12. Find two words which are synonyms. One word reads either clockwise or counter-clockwise around the outer circle and the other reads in the opposite direction in the inner circle. You must provide the missing letters.

13. STULTIFYING is to STUPEFYING as

PEDESTRIAN is to painful, ponderous, stereotyped, vacuous, parochial

14. Which is the odd one out?

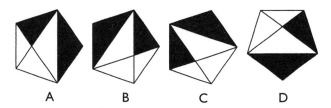

A   B   C   D

15. A B C D E F G H
Which letter is immediately to the right of the letter which is three to the left of the letter which is placed midway between the letter immediately to the left of the letter G and the letter immediately to the right of the letter A?

16. Find the two words that are closest in meaning:

pacify, mock, chaff, mob, mix, cool

17. Which is the odd one out?

traipse, sprint, perambulate, promenade, toddle

18. What word, when placed in the brackets, completes the first word and starts the second word?

NOSE (. . . .) WAGON

19. Which one of these is not a fruit?

TMUASAS
GLOATEN
IGABONE
DOOCVAA
KUINMPP

20. Place 3 two-letter bits together to equal a puzzle game.

LO   DO   GS   JI   TO   AW

21. Which word can be placed in front to make four new words?

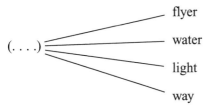

flyer
water
light
way

(. . . .)

22.

Which option below continues the above sequence?

A   B   C   D

23. Insert the word that means the same as the definitions outside the brackets.

plunder (. . . .) ancient wine

24. What is taupe? Is it:
- (a) a macaw
- (b) a large book
- (c) a brownish color
- (d) a pearl
- (e) a barn

25. Which is the odd one out?

dromond, sampan, barouche, whaler, caravel

26. Logically, which digit should replace the (?) ?
- (a) 6
- (b) 7
- (c) 8
- (d) 9
- (e) 0

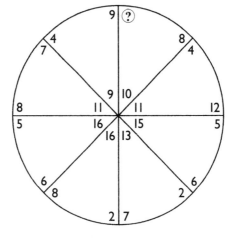

27. Which two words are closest in meaning?

cauldron, restaurant, brasserie, lingerie, barbecue, heliotrope

28. Find the item below that is always a part of:

NEGUS

shrimp, hot water, turnips, broccoli, semolina

29. Solve the anagram (one word).

SEEN AS MIST

utside George Norris's home in Spr
g they must have come to the wror
e shoved against a wall and friskec
officers ransacked his house. They
on the floor and eventually loaded

3/16/2011

30. How many different routes are there from A to B?

  (a) 8
  (b) 9
  (c) 10
  (d) 11
  (e) 12

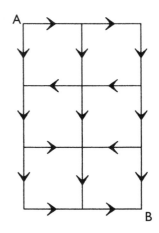

31. Complete the words which are synonyms, clockwise or counterclockwise.

32. Consider the following list of words:
  FREIGHTER, BONEYARD, DRIFTWOOD

Now choose just one of the following words which you think has most in common with them.
  SAIL, CANINE, OCEAN, WRECKAGE, RENDER

33. Find the word that means the same as:
  VACILLATE
  hesitate, vanish, depose, improve, oscillate

34. Which two words are opposite in meaning?
  trivial, renegade, coercion, loyalist, specious, celebrity

35. Which of these is not a wind?
  nimbus, mistral, zephyr, sirocco, hurricane

36.

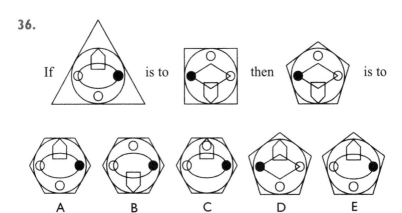

37. Which one of these is not a color?

RONWB
WOYELL
VUMAE
CLECY
SETRUS

38. Insert a word which completes the first word and starts the second word.

HOT (. . . .) STONE

39. Which of these is the odd one out?

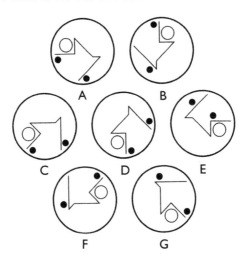

40. Which of the following is the missing tile?

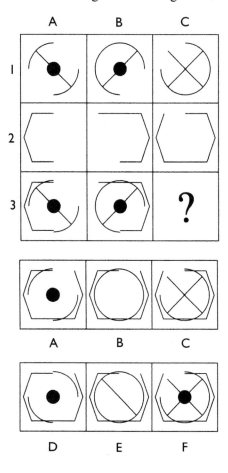

Test Eight *Answers*

1. B. The first three figures are repeated but cut in half and the left half only is shown.

2. wind: to produce tailwind and windbreak.

3. TUNIC:

₂ ₃ ₁ _{4 2 1 5 3} ₅ ₄
STIRRED (RIDER) CREEPER

₂ ₃ ₁ _{4 2 1 5 3} ₅ ₄
SOUPCON (TUNIC) UPRIGHT

4. angled

5. TONCOT = COTTON. The others are lamb, bread, butter, bacon.

6. CRUDE

7. C. The figure is repeated, but with curved lines straight and straight lines curved.

8. allowance

9. useless

10. invade, inveighed

11. B. One is a mirror image of the other, except that black and white are reversed.

12. ornament, decorate

13. ponderous

14. B. The others are the same figure rotated.

15. B

16. mock, chaff

17. sprint: sprint is to run, the rest are to walk.

18. band: to produce noseband and bandwagon.

19. IGABONE = BEGONIA. The fruits are satsuma, tangelo, avocado and pumpkin.

20. jigsaw

21. high

22. A. Large triangles are added to right and left in turn, first the right way up (one each side) then upside down. All area covered by more than one triangle is shaded.

23. sack

24. (c) a brownish color

25. barouche: it is a horse-drawn carriage, the others are all boats.

26. (c) 8. In each segment the sum of the two outside numbers equals the opposite central number.

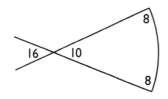

27. brasserie, restaurant

28. hot water

29. steaminess

30. (c) 10

31. scampish, improper

32. canine: it contains a number ca[nine] as do fr[eight]er, b[one]yard and drif[two]od

33. hesitate

34. renegade, loyalist

35. nimbus: a sort of cloud

36. A. The top and bottom symbols within the large circle switch round, as do the left and right symbols. The ellipse and the diamond shapes in the center also switch. The large circle stays the same, and the outer shape adds an extra side.

37. CLECY = CYCLE. The colors are brown, yellow, mauve, russet.

38. head

39. E. A is the same as C + D. B is the same as F + G.

40. C. Col A + Col. B = Col. C Line 1 + Line 2 = Line 3 Similar lines and symbols disappear.

Index